Wakefield Press

The Feeling of Bigness

Helen Parsons grew up in Adelaide and studied history and English literature at the University of Adelaide, where she completed an Honours Degree. After university she spent time in Europe, including a year of study in Italy and a year of work in London. Back in Adelaide she worked as a teacher of English as a second language, and later in the Australian office of *New Internationalist* magazine.

Her poems have been published in Australian and overseas journals.

The Feeling of Bigness

Encountering Georgia O'Keeffe

HELEN PARSONS

Wakefield Press
16 Rose Street
Mile End
South Australia 5031
www.wakefieldpress.com.au

First published 2020

Designed and typeset by Michael Deves, Wakefield Press

ISBN 978 1 74305 712 4

A catalogue record for this book is available from the National Library of Australia

Wakefield Press thanks Coriole Vineyards for continued support

For Hilary and Sue and Annie

'a week ago it was the mountains that I thought the most wonderful – and today it's the plains – I guess it's the feeling of bigness in both that just carries me away ...'

Letter from O'Keeffe to Stieglitz, 4 September 1916

'last night I felt myself into my heart, out of my head, and then became aware of this sense of self much bigger, unlimited, like the self in music ...'

Marion Milner, *An Experiment in Leisure*

Contents

Preface

Twenty years ago a friend lent me a biography of the American artist Georgia O'Keeffe. I was immediately engaged by Georgia's story: her determination to be independent and to speak her truth in her art, her passionate and difficult relationship with the photographer Alfred Stieglitz, her love for New Mexico.

It's not hard for someone who loves the often harsh landscapes of southern Australia to be drawn to the idea of New Mexico, and I had already been entranced by the descriptions of that country in the novels of Willa Cather.

A year or so later I travelled with my then partner to Washington DC where he had a work conference. We chanced upon an exhibition of O'Keeffe's paintings and Stieglitz's photographs. To see them in real life was a powerful experience. I started writing the poems then, though some may have begun to take shape earlier.

Some years later we went to the United States again, for a conference in Boston, and this time we also travelled to New Mexico. I saw places Georgia had painted and the house she had lived in.

Poems grew out of my reflections on Georgia's art and life, and on the ways her art and her story resonated with my own experiences. The poems turned into sonnets. The accumulation turned into a sequence. Here they are.

Breath

Air lifts the clamping rib-cage and makes space
around the beating heart. Air sighs and sings
as the bow moves across the tight-held strings.
And air inflates her tunic, tugs her hair,
billows and buffets her as she stands here
on the dry Texas plains. There's rapture
in this faded picture. Simply her,
high sky, a vast expanse of grass. And air.
In Botticelli's *Spring* the wreathing wind
breathes on a simple nymph so she's transformed
to Flora: from her lap and arms spill flowers,
in her cool and watchful face shines joy.
So Georgia now. And she'll draw lines as clear
as violin notes curving through the air.

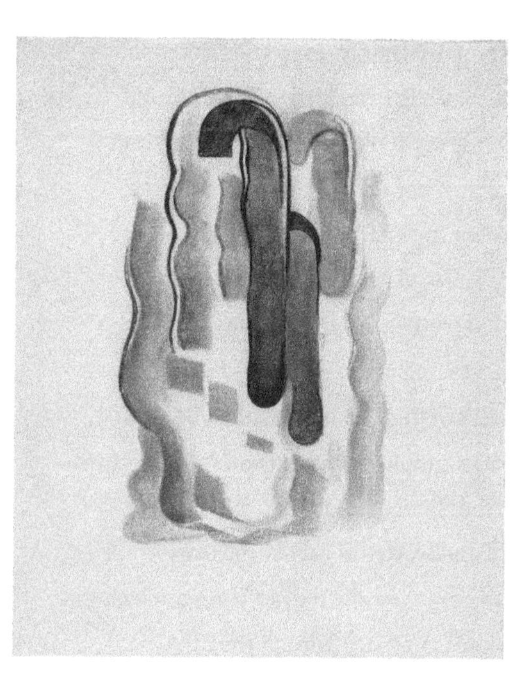

Charcoals

She walked into the sunset and then back
into the quiet town. She was unquiet,
wanting to sing the sunset and the night,
her restless blood, but to sing truthfully,
in cadences that came unforced, untrained.
She spread blank papers on the floor and crouched
before them. Ovoids and arcs appeared, spirals,
a line that rose and fell. The shadings moved
from palest grey to black. The charcoal was
as sensitive as mercury to fever
and feverishly she drew, and saw emerge
a syntax of her own, her syllables,
primal and strange, as if a mermaid sang
upon a darkening and mercurial sea.

Blessing

The narrative is never pure or simple
but some moments are. She posts her drawings
to the friend who carries them to Stieglitz,
he with the heart, the eye, the years of practice
in discernment. And he sees them, sees her
in them, affirms at once their truth and beauty.
There's a concerto where the cello leaves
the confines of its conversation with
the other instruments. Alone it speaks,
expressive, unconstrained, exposed.
Listening you hold your breath. Then like a wave
the orchestra returns: *Yes, this is right,*
it says, *and true, and more than good.*
The gift of this. The grace. The benediction.

Bed

Who would refuse enchantment? Siren song;
the Pentecostal mandate of a flame
descending; a possession, a release.
They are together now. They pull the bed
into the centre of the attic room
beneath the skylight. Sun and moon and stars
process above them, signalling to them
their innocence, their central place
within the scheme of things. Such certitude.
The room, small universe, holds other things:
his camera and its tripod, the black drape,
the dingy white umbrella that will serve
to hold and focus light. Her easel waits,
her canvases, his photographic plates.

GEORGIA O'KEEFFE
ALFRED STIEGLITZ

Book

The book of photographs – of course I bought it –
is large and elegant, thick ivory paper,
verso pages blank, a generous space
around each print. I was with you in Boston.
Windows framed grey sky but in the gallery shop
it was all gleam and glory. Music too:
one of the Strauss Last Songs, expansive, grand,
as if a ship sailed from a fjord out
upon the open sea. And so I felt,
and so I feel, remembering. The pages
blurred before my eyes. Why tears? Because
of music and of art. Because a bond
as difficult and doomed as ours could make
this moment and this monument, this beauty.

Resolution

She took upon herself his varied visions.
She served his art as priestess, holding still
for the long minutes needed as the shapes
impressed themselves upon the coated glass.
He turned his lens on every part of her:
the hollow of the collar-bone, the belly's
swell, the dark declivities, the creases
at the corner of an eye. His pictures
show her most and least herself, absolve her
of herself, resolve her. How we long
for resolution, revelation, form,
and here it is. The shutter clicks. Art lifts
the fleeting moments out of time.
We hold them still in images and rhyme.

Dissolution

This may be the one I love the most.
No artifice, no poses, just her face,
shadowed and softened, looking out at us.
No, not at us, at him. I know that look.
She's been dissolved by love and making love,
made simple, opened up by intimacy.
She who was guarded is unguarded here,
the boundaries are blurred. I think of Blake,
his *lineaments of gratified desire*,
which was, he said, what men and women want
from one another. Soulful animals.
There's melancholy here and merriment.
Despite the shadows something is transparent
and even luminous. She's fully present.

Woven

Washington was hard. Near our hotel
the bookshops, bars and cafes overflowed,
but the fountain in the square was dead and dry.
In its vast bowl lay shards of dingy ice
and ancient litter. You were frozen too.
I chanced upon a brochure in the lobby:
an exhibition from their first ten years,
his photographs, her paintings. So we walked
into the cold grey day and found the place.
Outside the entrance stood great woven forms
made out of willow branches, intertwined;
intricate structures not designed to last.
The wands were supple still and rosy-brown.
Up close they breathed the freshness of the woods.

Interwoven

All that would divide them later was
already there, held in abeyance by
desire and discovery and delusion,
and by the interweaving of their arts.
Those early years were charged with looking
at each other and the world and at each other's
looking at the world. They sought a music,
strove to catch the soul of things, the soul
in things, the life that comes to meet you
when you pay attention. Fallen leaves,
the canyon of a New York street, the clouds
above Lake George: inside the force-field
of their looking the opaque grew lucent
and the voiceless sang. As still it sings.

Crows

Sometimes she couldn't breathe.
The family intimacy, the heady talk
of friends and colleagues, cluttered up the space
of her expansive private way
of being in the world. An upstairs window
overlooked the lake and here she worked,
painted at this remove the smooth ellipse,
its deep and chalky variable blues,
the curving shore-line, the soft fringe
of closely-standing trees. Above the blue
three crows, black fragments, flap and float
in the big air. You can just see
along the painting's right-hand edge
the gauzy billow of a blowing curtain.

Alchemy

The room is large with sunlight, soft with dust.
The door is barred. She's taken over this shed
and here she works, intent, encircled by
her own hermetic space. The brush gleams purple.
Her attention moves from flower to canvas, back
again, again. Evening draws in. Outside
the lake grows dim. A single bird calls, then
the distant sound of laughter from the house
as people gather, the familiar flock.
She wipes her brushes and prepares to leave.
The living blooms are limp, have folded in
upon themselves, but from the painting gaze
their dark green eyes. As she walks to the house,
she feels herself the lake that holds the moon.

Kali

Yet sometimes something seems disjointed,
crude. A lurid colouration jars the eye,
a jagged line irrupts. Harsh as a trumpet
in a harmony of strings and shocking
as her slap upon a child's smooth cheek.
This cloud evokes a tenderness, it is
so undulant and soft. The twilight sky
of greenish blue has depth and drift.
But the red band of the hills feels violent,
overdone, and there's a streak that slashes
through the painting like a super-highway.
So Kali strides upon the scene, fierce-eyed
and garlanded with skulls, the Dark One,
forcing an entry and demanding worship.

Private

What her body said in private her paintings
sang in public: openings and beckonings,
the rise and fall, the stretch and arch, the rapture.
That's how they read her flower and music paintings.
She hated all the nudging and the smudging.
Just flowers, she said, just music, lines and colours.
But flowers are sex, music is of the flesh,
and close attention calls up Eros. Fire
ignites beneath a glass that magnifies.
She came in close, impelled. The iris showed
its dark reveals, the lily opened, poppies
blazed. And she described them in her clear
calligraphy, her hard-won alphabet,
her own exposed and naked idiolect.

Public

That afternoon in Santa Fe we wandered
through the gallery. Our footsteps echoed
on the polished floors. Our talk was hushed.
After a while you said that she was better
than you'd thought. I don't know what I said.
Her goodness was not new to me, nor was
her badness. Surprising was the shock I felt
watching the clothed and casual men walk past
those open flowers and those naked landscapes.
It came to me that some rooms should be private,
for women only, or for initiates in
some mystery. Crazy of course. Where would you
draw the line? Black door? White cliff? Eros
takes many forms. I'm just saying how I felt.

Shell

Before the deserts of the south there was
the northern sea. Before the bones, the shells.
Her weeks alone in Maine caused Alfred grief
but she stayed on there, stubborn and entranced.
The shell she paints is clear. No frill of weed
disturbs the polished carapace. It closes:
muscled hinges pull the wings together
and the seam holds fast. You may admire
the contours of this armour; you'll see nothing
through the narrow chinks. And then it opens
to reveal its colours: pale blue, pearl grey,
a wash of yellow, the faint flush of rose.
How subtle is the landscape it contains,
as fresh and spacious as the southern plains.

Story

She is not blind. She sees she is being pushed
off to one side. This woman's smooth and sweet,
child-like, a woman with a child. Her breasts
brim milk, her eyes brim with devotion.
There is no means of fighting this. Besides,
Georgia has cultivated distance, held
herself apart, and now she's caught.
She tries to think her way out of this corner
but her brain's as stiff as her unbending back,
useless now before the march of things.
Her face grows blank with puzzlement and pride,
and shame is like a stopper in her throat.
Her story's thickening, taking a new shape,
but it is not the shape that she had wanted.

Stone

She's waning now, body and spirit thin.
Another narrative is gaining ground.
How is she to move back to the centre
of her story? And how are we to read it?
Happy for him that he has found this comfort?
For Dorothy, that she has found a cause?
Content for Georgia too? For this will free her,
force her into the wilderness, her home.
Or do we judge him as a foolish vain
old man, and Dorothy a narcissist,
naïve and needy? Georgia then? Perhaps
she's hard, like the smooth stones she painted
in the picture called *My heart*. Many would say
she brought it on herself. A difficult woman.

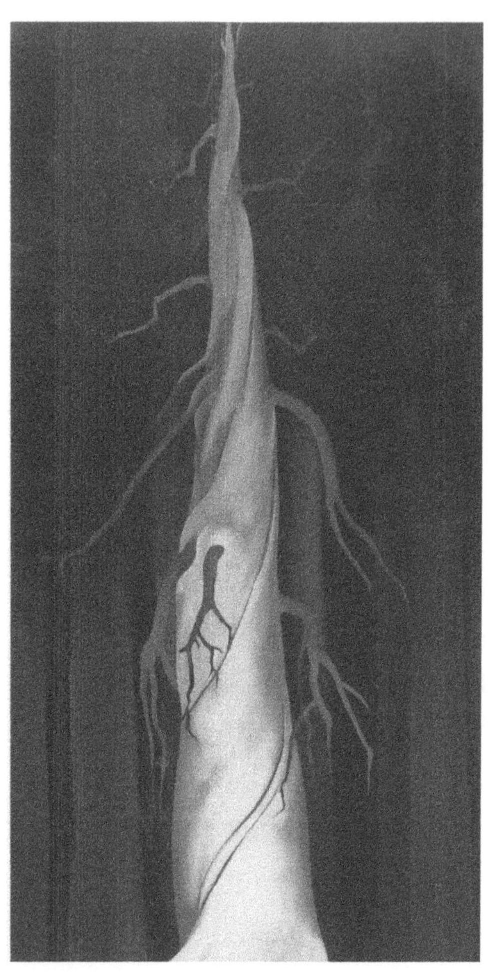

Sister

Unreasonable and unkind. Of course.
It's savage, sisterhood. How hard she'd fought
through youth to keep her clarity, her edge,
and then, when she lay ill and lapped by doubt,
the news came from her sturdy younger sister
of a first exhibition, flower paintings,
close-ups, rich-hued. It was an axe-blow
to the roots. No, worse, it drew her back
into the forest, family's dark wood,
where she was just another variation
on a theme, she who had worked so hard
to find her ground, her theme. So she struck out.
It was not reasoned, not cold cruelty.
She was both lightning and the blasted tree.

Snow

Years back I saw a documentary film
about a writer. What has stayed with me
is this one image: after her daughter's death
she went to bed each night with coats and wraps
heaped heavy over her so she could sleep.
I think of this when I am reading of
the vast exhaustion that laid Georgia low
at intervals throughout her long long life:
the months after her mother's death, and then
the year when art and Alfred both betrayed her.
Fragile, recovering, she painted barns,
bandaged in whiteness, blanketed in snow,
the silent shining weight a kind of comfort,
a way of wintering out, awaiting spring.

Sun

Bermuda then. Beside the banyan tree
she lay for hours, staring at the clouds,
those shape-changers, while the old thoughts,
weary, worn thin, circled about her brain.
As they dissolved she floated in the clear
and simple blue. The sun warmed more than skin.
Almost a smile softened her face. A sigh.
Leaves wavered, sucked up light. The tree
reached out its aerial roots. The nerve of it
impressed her, how it flung those fibrous ropes.
She reached for charcoal, paper, and began
with unaccustomed hand to sketch the bole,
the shoots, the way they dangled in thin air,
the way they grew by instinct towards the earth.

Earth

I plant a pear tree in my city garden.
Deep hole, dark crumbly earth, the ball of roots
fanned out a little, a slow watering.
Such images came naturally to her,
of earth and elements and cultivation.
At first with Stieglitz she had felt herself
a nurtured plant. Then came the desolation.
Later, recovering, she told a friend
she'd learned she had to guard her ground,
protect that fertile inner space. She'd not
allow there any growth that was not native,
nor risk neglect, nor have it wrecked again.
I'm thinking of her as I work my square of soil.
The green leaves wave against the western wall.

Car

She's bought a car, her first. It's black.
It waits for her beside the kerb. It's faithful.
Its clean lines curve as lovely as a flower
but it is armour, engine, invitation.
Her spirits rise as she inhales the tonic
fragrances of petrol, metal, leather.
She wakes its power when she turns the key.
Her eyes flick up and sideways, checking behind.
She's changing gear now, awkwardly at first
but then each time a smoother modulation.
She feels her body settling on the seat.
Her hands upon the wheel are useful again.
The city is a dream of crowds and noise.
She is American: the country opens before her.

Cross

She wouldn't have been thinking about
penitence. I might have been but she,
I think, was pitting herself against the vastness
of that landscape. I imagine her paints
stiffening in the cold bright air and her
standing, unsure, shut out, her eye
being drawn then to the tall wooden cross,
the Penitente cross. She'd heard the tales
of that self-flagellating sect; for her though
the dark cross was a call towards nothing
but the shapes space took in this new world.
She straightened, squeezed black paint upon the board,
set the cross against the sky, a view-finder,
and raised her brush as carefully as a gun.

Artefact

Their lives have split apart but still they spend
the winter months, those short dark days, together.
And their connection has become a myth
for both of them, a structure that lives on.
I saw a ziggurat of beeswax once,
a tall stepped edifice of dullish gold,
breathing the faintest scent of honey through
the gallery. The liquid sweetness
that had lived within the comb was gone.
The energy that flowed between them, gleamed
in photographs and paintings, has lapsed now.
From what remains they mould this artefact:
a keep-sake for the sake of keeping faith,
as truthful and delusive as a myth.

House

She found a crumbling house upon a hill
and bought it, had the mud-brick walls restored,
the final layer smoothed by women's hands
in keeping with the Indian tradition,
so all was textured, tactile, porous, curved,
with kiva hearths carved into earthen walls
and plain wide ledges under plain wide windows.
Beneath the timbered ceilings globes hung bare.
But one among the rooms stayed roofless always,
open to light and air, awake to shadows.
There she could stand beneath the arching sky,
tilt back her head and see the clouds, the stars.
A bird could build a nest there. Just imagine.
A nest of clay against the smooth clay wall.

Garden

Three acres inside high adobe walls
are her domain, and like a Mogul lord
she turns to make a garden now within
the new-secured realm. A private paradise.
Provident too for she's a farmer's daughter:
the rose is set amid the circling onions,
poppies bloom beside the salad greens.
And everywhere is order. There's a grid
of irrigation channels, narrow paths.
The feathery tamarisks are pruned,
the strappy iris leaves cut back.
Like a Zen priest she walks in her black garb.
Upon the planks that lid the well she rests
some shapely stones. A shifting meditation.

Window

It’s bare, spare in its plantings, soil as dry
as the ridged bark of the dusty tamarisks.
The fibrous iris leaves are clipped and browning.
I walk raised paths beside the gutters dug
to carry rationed water to low beds.
Here she would have stood on summer evenings,
watching the slow flood, smelling the wet earth.
We look through windows at her bedroom:
walls the blue-grey of a heron’s wing,
white cotton spread over the single bed.
The wide glass also holds the landscape,
reflects the sweep of valley, cliffs and sky.
And I’m there too, a slender dark
transparency. I see myself as I look in.

Change

The new cosmology, post menopause:
the pelvis floats against the sky. There is
a buoyancy about it. At its edge
the moon's pale circle waits, a ghostly egg.
But this womb is a lake of emptiness,
a tunnel of blue air. I think of how
I grieved and raged at that great loss:
loss of the tension and the lapse, the tides,
the fluid evidence of something
going on, a basic life that persevered
no matter how stuck head and heart might be.
I wonder how she felt. The painting seems
so calm about the change, so open to
ethereal rhythms, an expanding sky.

Door

In middle age I feel the burden of my goods.
I am a boat so barnacled it lists,
founders in shallow tides. I long to gaze
on a blank wall, to watch the shadows shift
on it. Or else to look at her black door.
She bought the house for that, she said, that door,
and she restored the house around it. Bare
adobe walls, a courtyard space of sand and sage.
Her paintings show it fixed in the bright air,
but almost lifting, peeling off the canvas,
a dazzling darkness held within its square.
It calls to me. It beckons and it bars.
It is the tunnel in the needle's eye.
It is the pupil of her eye, unblinking.

Dog

She lives alone, but now there is the dog.
Another source of warmth, another pulse,
another creature breathing, dreaming, moving
through this space that she controls.
Another pair of eyes regards the world
but blessedly there is no commentary,
no talk to pull her from her reveries,
distract her from herself. Meticulous
she brushes the thick pelt. In its warm fleece
the dog sits at the open door and looks
upon the falling snow, becomes a piece
of quietness within the spreading quiet.
Black dog, white world. And then the pattern breaks.
Its fur is spangled now with shining flakes.

Smoke

The resin smell of pinyon smoke entranced us,
sharp and sweet in Santa Fe's dark streets.
The room we stayed in had a fireplace,
a kiva's arching hollow in the mud-
brick wall, a foot or so above the floor.
The pale dry wood stood conically stacked
and flamed up at the first touch of a match.
The winters on that high plateau get cold.
At night she would have had the fire burning;
maybe music played, her Monteverdi
or her Bach. Perhaps she simply listened
to the quiet, sometimes perhaps stepped out,
to see the risen moon, the scattered stars,
to smell that fragrant drift upon the air.

Salvage

She's living in a world of shadows now,
vision peripheral and colour gone.
It happened gradually, the fading out.
She looks across the plain towards the mountain,
the Pedernàl's truncated cone, so often
painted. Can you see it? asks the friend.
I can't, she answers, but I know it's there.
So faith and memory must compose her views.
And there is touch. She sits beside the window.
Even the sun's full light can't clarify
the shapes that blur before her clouded eyes.
Dry river stones lie spread and tumbled
on the sill. Her wrinkled hands read
the smooth surfaces, feed the old hunger.

Dependence

The child's blind trust is a necessity,
a part of its odd armoury of survival.
In old age's second childhood where
was she to trust? She had her money, ample
to pay servants and maintain the house.
Her hands could reassure her of the world:
the dog's warm fur, the iris's broad blade.
But she was growing frail. Her nerve had weakened.
And then there was the heart, the needful heart,
that in the lucky child is met with love.
Into her cooling world now stepped
a warm young man. Buying his bullying care
she was half adult and controlling still,
half child, unseeing and compelled to trust.

Death

There needs to be a poem about her death,
which came at last. She had outlived her life,
was biding time, was waiting for the body
to give up, give out, give over. She was never
one for giving in. She had become
a legend. On the desert's earthen floor
she'd laid the woven carpet of her life,
and like the rugs the Indians wove it held
a spirit-line, a break in the design,
a flaw. A way to separate the maker
from the made, a dark and narrow door
through which the soul could slide and find its way
back to the bigger life: the sky, the stars,
the aromatic air, the waiting earth.

Eccentric

Fear is the great unbalancer. Always
she lived with it, she said. It was a presence,
like the rattle snakes that hid up in the hills.
How beautiful their chained and curving spines.
She gathered them and put one under glass,
a talisman upon the coffee-table.
What then steeled her spine? What kept her upright?
Desire, and the discipline of work,
and her eccentric path.
                                        Eccentric,
how it sways, that word, then balances
in its clear consonants. At dusk she walked
along the ridge-tops, her dark figure small
in that bare landscape, centred in its breadth,
her being infused with its sage-scented breath.

Notes

This sequence of poems draws primarily on Roxana Robinson's biography *Georgia O'Keeffe*, Bloomsbury, 1990.

Breath

In 1912 O'Keeffe, aged 25, went to Amarillo, Texas to teach art. This was her first encounter with the American South West.

Charcoals

In 1915 O'Keeffe began a new series of personal works, abstractions drawn in charcoal.

Blessing

In 1916 Anita Pollitzer showed her friend's drawings to Alfred Stieglitz, famous photographer and leading figure in the New York art world. He exhibited them in his gallery and began a correspondence with O'Keeffe.

Bed

In 1918 O'Keeffe left her teaching position in Texas and moved to New York where she pursued painting full-time. Stieglitz left his marriage of 25 years to live with her. He began his photographic portrait of her at this time.

Book

Georgia O'Keeffe: A Portrait by Alfred Stieglitz, Metropolitan Museum of Art, New York, 1978; revised edition 1997.

Crows

Stieglitz and his extended family traditionally spent the summers at Lake George, near New York.

Alchemy

O'Keeffe and friends fixed up an old out-building of the Lake George house to provide her with a private studio space.

Private

O'Keeffe's first solo exhibition, New York, 1923.

Public

The Georgia O'Keeffe Museum, Santa Fe, New Mexico; opened 1997.

Shell

Open Clam Shell and *Closed Clam Shell,* oil paintings 1927.

Story

From 1929 onwards Dorothy Norman, young married socialite and patron of the arts, played an increasingly important part in Stieglitz's life.

Sisterhood

In 1933 O'Keeffe's younger sister Catherine exhibited her paintings. O'Keeffe responded to news of this with a letter of such fury that Catherine never painted again.

Earth

'My center does not come from my mind – it feels in me like a plot of warm moist well-tilled earth ...' Letter from Georgia O'Keeffe to Jean Toomer 1933, quoted in Robinson, p. 399.

Cross

O'Keeffe made her first journey to New Mexico in 1929. This began a pattern of summers spent painting there.

Door

O'Keeffe bought an abandoned adobe house in Abiqiu in 1945 and had it restored. She settled there permanently after Stieglitz's death in 1946. The phrase 'a dazzling darkness' is taken from Henry Vaughan's poem 'The Night'.

Dog

There are two photographs by Myron Wood of O'Keeffe's chow dogs and the falling snow in the book *O'Keeffe at Abiqiu.* (Harry N. Abrams, 1995)

Change

Pelvis with moon, oil painting 1943.

Salvage

In 1971 O'Keeffe began to lose her central vision due to macular degeneration.

Dependence

In 1973 Juan Hamilton, a young potter, entered O'Keeffe's life. Over the following years his care and attention became increasingly important to her, and his role in her life more central.

Death

O'Keeffe died in 1986, aged 99. Her ashes were scattered in northern New Mexico.

List of illustrations

28 **Cross**
Black Cross with Stars and Blue
1929
Oil paint on canvas
40 × 30 in; 101.6 × 76.2 cm
Private Collection
© Georgia O'Keeffe Museum/ARS. Copyright Agency, 2020

32 **Garden**
Myron Wood
Wellhead cover
Photographs taken between 1979 and 1982
From the book *O'Keeffe at Abiquiu* by Christine Taylor Patten
Harry N. Abrams, Publishers, New York, 1995
Held in the Myron Wood Collection in
Pikes Peak Library District
Copyright © Pikes Peak Library District

36 **Door**
Patio with cloud
1956
Oil on canvas
36 × 30 in. (91.44 × 76.2 cm)
Milwaukee Art Museum
© Georgia O'Keeffe Museum/ARS. Copyright Agency, 2020

40 **Salvage**
Myron Wood
A Rock Collection
Photograph taken between 1979 and 1982
From the book *O'Keeffe At Abiquiu* by Christine Taylor Patten
Harry N. Abrams, Publishers, New York, 1995
Held in the Myron Wood Collection in
Pikes Peak Library District
Copyright © Pikes Peak Library District

44 Eccentric

John Loengard
Georgia O'Keeffe on evening walk with her dogs, Ghost Ranch, 1966
The LIFE Picture Collection via Getty Images

Cover image

Georgia in Texas
From *Georgia O'Keefe: A Biography*, Roxana Robinson, Bloomsbury, London, 1990.
Photograph courtesy of Catherine Krueger (Georgia O'Keeffe's niece).

Acknowledgements

My thanks to the editors of the following publications in which some of these poems or earlier versions of them first appeared: *Meanjin, Antipodes, Australian Poetry Journal, Blue Dog, Famous Reporter, Island, Cordite Poetry Review,* the *Australian* and the *Age.*

Thanks

The gestation of this collection has been long and many people have given me encouragement along the way. Hilary Parsons and Suzanne Gebhardt have been unwavering in their faith. Louise Nicholas and Helen Lindstrom have always been ready with support and counsel. Jan Owen and Diane Fahey have been invaluable mentors, and I have appreciated their attentiveness and generosity more than I can say.

I am grateful to the members of Jan Owen's poetry workshops for their feedback and fellowship.

Heart-felt thanks go also to Pamela Evers, Bob Gibson, and Narelle McKenzie.

And thank you to Michael Deves who has helped so much with the process of publication.

Wakefield Press is an independent publishing and distribution company based in Adelaide, South Australia. We love good stories and publish beautiful books. To see our full range of books, please visit our website at www.wakefieldpress.com.au where all titles are available for purchase. To keep up with our latest releases, news and events, subscribe to our monthly newsletter.

Find us!

Facebook: www.facebook.com/wakefield.press
Twitter: www.twitter.com/wakefieldpress
Instagram: www.instagram.com/wakefieldpress

www.ingramcontent.com/pod-product-compliance
Ingram Content Group Australia Pty Ltd
76 Discovery Rd, Dandenong South VIC 3175, AU
AUHW020940111125
419315AU00003B/46

9 781743 057124